FEB 2017

D1367247

Rookie
Read-About®
Science

Freaky Fish

by Lisa M. Herrington

Content Consultant
Dr. Lucy Spelman
Zoological Medicine Specialist

Reading Consultant
Jeanne M. Clidas, Ph.D.
Reading Specialist

Children's Press®
An Imprint of Scholastic Inc.

Library of Congress Cataloging-in-Publication Data
Herrington, Lisa M., author.
Freaky fish/by Lisa M. Herrington.
    pages cm. — (Rookie read about science. Strange animals)
Summary: "Introduces the reader to freaky fish." — Provided by publisher.
Includes index.
ISBN 978-0-531-22601-8 (library binding) — ISBN 978-0-531-22747-3 (pbk.)
    1. Fishes—Miscellanea—Juvenile literature. 2. Children's questions and answers.
I. Title.
QL617.2.H47 2016
    597.02—dc23   2015021145

Produced by Spooky Cheetah Press
Design by Keith Plechaty

© 2016 by Scholastic Inc.

Printed in China 62

SCHOLASTIC, CHILDREN'S PRESS, ROOKIE READ-ABOUT®, and associated logos
are trademarks and/or registered trademarks of Scholastic Inc.

1 2 3 4 5 6 7 8 9 10 R 25 24 23 22 21 20 19 18 17 16

Photographs ©: cover: Laura Dinraths; 3 top left: Awashima Marine Park/Getty
Images; 3 top right: skynesher/iStockphoto; 3 bottom: Makoto Kanzaki/Minden
Pictures; 4 background: nevodka/Shutterstock, Inc.; 4 main: GlobalP/iStockphoto;
7 background: nevodka/Shutterstock, Inc.; 7 main: NaturePL/Superstock, Inc.; 8:
Rich Carey/Shutterstock, Inc.; 11 top: Olga Khoroshunova/Dreamstime; 11 bottom:
Stubblefieldphoto/Dreamstime; 12: Shin Okamoto/Getty Images; 15: Reinhard
Dirscherl/Getty Images; 16: Colin Parker/National Geographic Creative; 19 top:
Reinhard Dirscherl/Getty Images; 19 bottom: Piotr Wawrzyniuk/Dreamstime; 20:
Danté Fenolio/Science Source; 23: Minden Pictures/Superstock, Inc.; 24: MBARI;
26: Rich Carey/Shutterstock, Inc.; 27: twospeeds/Shutterstock, Inc.; 28 background:
nevodka/Shutterstock, Inc.; 28 top: Michael Patrick O'Neill/Science Source; 28
bottom: Tom Stack/age fotostock; 29 background: nevodka/Shutterstock, Inc.; 29
top: Kristina Vackova/Shutterstock, Inc.; 29 center: NaturePL/Superstock, Inc.; 29
bottom: Minden Pictures/Superstock, Inc.; 30 background: nevodka/Shutterstock,
Inc.; 30 main: Minden Pictures/Superstock, Inc.; 31 top: Shin Okamoto/Getty
Images; 31 center top: Rich Carey/Shutterstock, Inc.; 31 center bottom: Bill Kennedy/
Shutterstock, Inc.; 31 bottom: Minden Pictures/Superstock, Inc.:

Table of Contents

That's Freaky!

Fish are fascinating! They come in all shapes, sizes, and colors—from a tiny goldfish to a huge shark. Fish can also be some of the freakiest creatures in the world.

For example, the porcupinefish has a unique secret.

Surprise! That cute little fish just blew up like a balloon. That is what it does when danger is near. First the porcupinefish swallows a lot of water. Then it swells up into a large prickly ball. **Predators** will not eat it now.

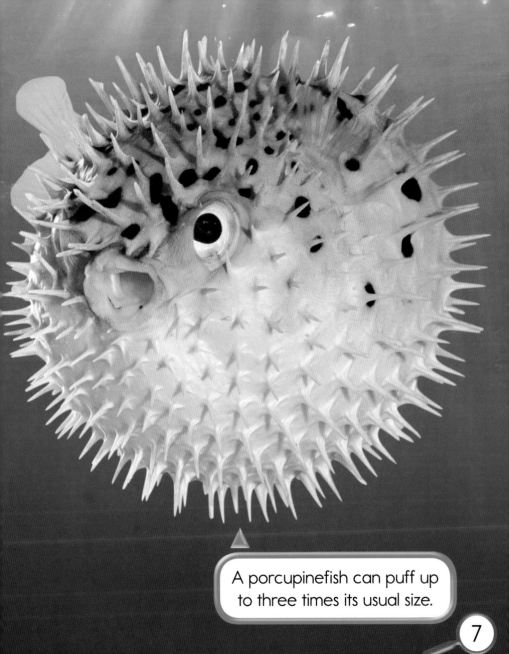

A porcupinefish can puff up to three times its usual size.

What Makes a Fish a Fish?

has a backbone

lives in water

most have tails

most use fins to swim

most breathe with gills

All fish live underwater. They all have backbones.

Most fish have **fins** to help them swim. Almost all of them use their **gills** to breathe underwater. And most of them have tails.

This parrotfish's mouth looks like a beak. The fish uses it to chew hard foods like coral.

Stay Away, Enemies

Most fish are covered with scales or bony plates. These are often hard and slippery.

The cowfish and boxfish have hard plates. They protect the fish from enemies. These funny-looking fish are also coated with a poisonous slime.

FUN FACT!

Some fish, such as moray eels, do not have scales. Morays have thick skin that is covered in mucus. That makes the eel feel smooth.

cowfish

boxfish

leafy sea dragon

Fish often use **camouflage**. That helps them blend in with their surroundings. The leafy sea dragon uses its shape as camouflage. It looks just like seaweed! Other fish cannot spot it among the plants.

FUN FACT!

Sea horses are unusual in a special way! Mother sea horses give their eggs to the fathers. The dads carry the eggs in a pouch until the babies are born.

Some fish have colors and patterns that show they are unsafe to eat. The lionfish's stripes warn enemies to stay away. Its sharp spines are filled with poison!

Other poisonous fish are brightly colored. This tells predators that these fish do not taste good!

When the lionfish feels threatened, it spreads its spines.

The whale shark's huge mouth stretches almost as wide as its body.

What's for Dinner?

Open wide! The whale shark is the biggest fish in the world. It can grow as big as a bus! The whale shark looks scary. But it is very gentle. It eats mostly tiny plants and animals.

FUN FACT!

Whale sharks have lots of tiny teeth. But they do not really use them. Instead, they suck in food through their gills and mouths.

Many fish have tricky ways
to snatch a meal. They make
themselves seem invisible!
The scary stargazer buries itself
in sand. Then it waits to gobble up
a smaller fish. Flounder and other
flatfish disappear on the ocean
floor. They lie there until a meal
swims by.

stargazer

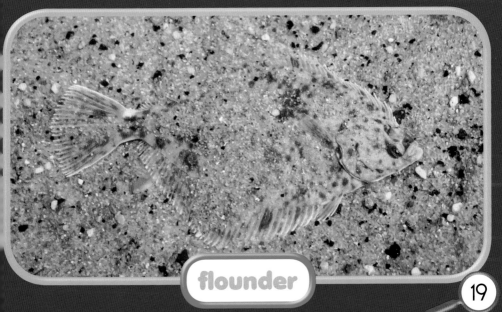

flounder

The deep sea is home to many freaky fish. The ocean is cold and totally dark there. Food is hard to find. The fish there have huge mouths. They will eat just about anything.

The viper fish has fangs so big that it cannot close its mouth.

Some deep-sea fish have a light called a lure. It dangles in front of the fish's mouth. When other fish come by to check it out, they are quickly gobbled up.

The anglerfish's light attracts a young fangtooth.

FUN FACT!

No one knew why the barreleye looks so strange. Then researchers at the Monterey Bay Aquarium Research Institute solved the mystery. The see-through head lets the fish look straight up to find prey overhead.

Fishy Finds

There are more than 30,000 kinds of fish. Scientists are discovering new ones all the time. Some of the strangest are found in the deep ocean. For example, the barreleye has a see-through head.

There is no doubt about it. Many fish really are freaky!

Which Is Stranger?

frogfish

- Frogfish often walk on their fins to move.
- Frogfish change colors to blend in with their surroundings. This helps them catch food.
- A frogfish's mouth can expand as wide as its body when it is catching a meal.

You Decide!

mudskipper

- Mudskippers can walk on land and breathe air. They can also skip and jump!

- Mudskippers have big eyes. These fish have sharp vision when they are out of the water.

- A mudskipper's front fins work like stubby legs.

TOP 5 Facts
About Fish

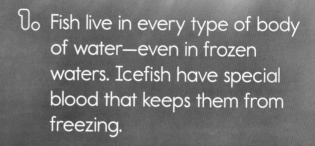

1. Fish live in every type of body of water—even in frozen waters. Icefish have special blood that keeps them from freezing.

2. Most fish swim by moving side to side. But some large fish, such as manta rays, move their fins up and down to swim.

3. Fish usually lay eggs in the water. Some fish, like sharks, give birth to live young. The male jawfish carries its eggs in its mouth until they hatch.

4. Many fish swim in groups called schools to stay safe from predators.

5. Flying fish burst out of the water with great speed. They use their fins to glide through the air.

Record Holders

Most Toxic
The stonefish has poison-packed spines on its body.

Fastest
The Atlantic sailfish can swim as fast as a car!

Most Eggs
The ocean sunfish can lay about 300 million eggs at a time!

Animal CRACK-UPS

Is this batfish wearing lipstick? No! Its lips are brightly colored to attract prey toward its mouth. Batfish are not very good swimmers. They use their fins to walk on the seafloor.

JOKES

1. **Where do fish sleep?**

2. **What do most fish and doctor's offices have in common?**

Answers: 1. On a seabed! 2. They have scales!

Glossary

camouflage (KAM-uh-flahzh): when an animal uses color, pattern, or shape to blend in with its surroundings

fins (FINS): body parts on a fish that are shaped like flaps and are used for swimming

gills (GILS): body parts on a fish that it uses to breathe

predators (PRED-uh-turs): animals that hunt other animals for food

Index

Facts for Now

Visit this Scholastic Web site for more information on fish:
www.factsfornow.scholastic.com
Enter the keyword **Fish**

About the Author

Lisa M. Herrington loves writing books about animals for kids. She lives in Trumbull, Connecticut, with her husband, daughter, and two not-so-freaky goldfish.